A GUIDE TO

Historic Virginia City

This book was made possible in part by funding
from the Montana Cultural Trust and
Virginia City's resort tax fund.

Montana Mainstreets

VOLUME ONE

A GUIDE TO
HISTORIC VIRGINIA CITY

by MARILYN GRANT

WITH A PREFACE BY
Paul Putz, State Historic Preservation Officer of Montana

AND AN AFTERWORD BY
John D. Ellingsen, Curator of Virginia City

COVER IMAGE: Looking south up Jackson Street, Virginia City, circa 1865
COVER DESIGN Kathryn Fehlig
BOOK DESIGN Arrow Graphics, Missoula
TYPESET IN Stempel Schneidler

All illustrations are from the collections of the
Montana Historical Society Photograph Archives, Helena,
unless otherwise noted.

MONTANA
CULTURAL
TRUST
Partial funding for this project was provided by Montana's Cultural Trust

ISBN-10: 0-917298-56-X
ISBN-13: 978-0-917298-56-1

LIBRARY OF CONGRESS CATALOGING-IN PUBLICATION DATA

Grant, Marilyn, 1932–
    Guide to historic Virginia City / Marilyn Grant.
        p.   cm. — (Montana mainstreets : v. 1)
    Includes bibliographical references.
    ISBN 0-917298-56-X (alk. paper)
    1. Virginia City (Mont.)—Guidebooks. 2. Virginia City (Mont.)—History.
    3. Historic buildings—Montana—Virginia City—Guidebooks. I. Titles. II. Series.
    F739.V5G72   1998
    917.86'663—dc21   98-29738
                                                    CIP

Contents

Preface

THIS BOOK, the first in a series of guidebooks to historic communities in Montana, derives much of its information from research and inventories conducted through the State Historic Preservation Office to find properties eligible for listing on the National Register of Historic Places. The Register lists places important to national, state, and local history and recognizes neighborhoods, commercial areas, individual sites, and even landscapes to call attention to the role they played in the history of our nation.

The National Register's founders understood that local history was the foundation of our nation's heritage and that a National Register of Historic Places would be incomplete without locally significant sites. The criteria for registration span a broad range of possibilities: the Register includes sites associated with important people; those of unique, masterful, or representative construction; and those that illuminate broad historical patterns. Significant, too, are those places such as archaeological sites containing information contributing to our understanding of history and prehistory. Within this range it is possible to construct the story of the United States, the rich interrelationship of its peoples, the incredible dynamism of its inhabitants through the ages, and the expression of its revolutionary ideals.

Your tour of this community will be a tour of the past, an examination of how the town grew, who built it, what economic factors sustained it, and how the community evolved socially. It will be a tour of history in a local context. Of course, the history of our nation continues to unfold, but usually only places older than fifty years are eligible for listing on the National Register. For that reason, you will not find our more recent history in the annals of the Register or much of it between these pages. Nor, in this guide, will you find mention of every building or incident significant to this community. Much research remains to be done on our Montana towns. Many historic sites and neighborhoods that deserve recognition remain to be researched and recorded in the Register.

This book will introduce you to certain noteworthy sites. But because there is much more in this community worthy of investigation than this volume can cover, this guidebook series is also designed to help you learn how to read for yourself the history written on a town's streets in brick, board, and stone. Within this volume are descriptions of many visible, expressive, and delightful sites and an abundance of compelling stories. May they launch you into a continuing exploration of the history that surrounds us all.

Paul Putz
State Historic Preservation
Officer of Montana

How to Use This Guide

VIRGINIA CITY was designated a National Historic Landmark in 1961 and was listed on the National Register of Historic Places in 1976 because of its contributions to western development and, more specifically, because of its status as an important 1860s gold-mining town during Montana Territory's gold rush days. The present-day visual significance of the town rests in mining sites and numerous preserved buildings that date from Virginia City's founding in 1863 through the 1890s.

Today's visitors see the leavings of increasingly efficient mining technology that forever marked the countryside surrounding Virginia City. In the town's homes and shops visitors see details of the western vernacular building style that developed during the nineteenth century as well as the influence of architectural styles popular in the East before and during the height of Virginia City's settlement. The evidence imprinted by earlier residents on the countryside and buildings reveals the history of Virginia City and explains how this one mining community fits into the pattern of western development.

The object of this guidebook is to help visitors learn to read the town's history as it was written in log, board, stone, and brick buildings and in the churned earth at mining claims. The guide points to clues on buildings and landscape that provide the visual evidence visitors need to interpret the story of

1

Virginia City's development. The book does not tell the whole story of Virginia City, nor does it take visitors on a site-by-site walking tour. The book is an interactive guide that enables visitors to be their own tour guides by helping them read the landscape through historical information, descriptive material, maps, and photographs.

The book's first section is a general overview that places Virginia City in the historical context of the western gold-mining frontier that moved into Montana in the mid-1860s. The overview focuses primarily on the town's most important years of mining, government, and commercial activity from 1863 to 1876.

The second section describes Virginia City buildings and mining sites representative of three periods of development in a typical western gold-mining town, again focusing on the years 1863 to 1876. A few buildings from the 1880s and 1890s are described because of the significance of their owners or because of their distinctive architectural features. Descriptions of mining activity are limited to placer sites on the town's western fringes. Although underground hard-rock mining contributed greatly to the region's economy, it was the 1860 gold rush days of placer mining that determined the town's character.

The best way to use the guide is to read it cover to cover before you begin your tour and carefully examine the maps on pages 4–5, 15, and 60. Check through the list of buildings and mining sites to orient yourself. As you walk along refer to the street map and site numbers that begin on page 4. It is important to remember that Virginia City continues to change, as it has for 135 years. Preservation of the town's historic buildings is ongoing. New construction continues, as well.

When you are familiar with Virginia City and know what to look for, you will begin to notice throughout the town and surrounding countryside architectural elements and mining remains similar to those described in this book. By applying the information in the guidebook to sites not specifically mentioned, you will be able to direct your own tour through this vibrant, living history site and increase your appreciation of this gold-mining town's history.

If this guidebook piques your interest in Virginia City's history, a bibliography on page 70 suggests additional reading that tells the region's story in greater detail.

This book benefited from the work of many people. The author would particularly like to thank Ellen Baumler, John Ellingsen, Lon Johnson, and Ken Sievert.

Visitors are reminded that Virginia City is a living, working community as well as a historic site. Many of the structures listed in this guide are privately owned. Residents are proud of their town and welcome your interest in its treasures. Please respect their privacy as you enjoy their hospitality.

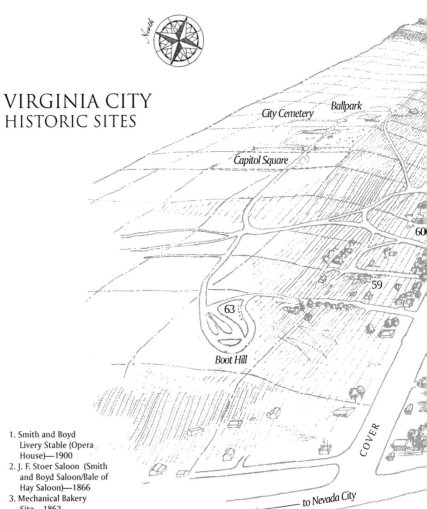

VIRGINIA CITY
HISTORIC SITES

North

City Cemetery   *Ballpark*

Capitol Square

60

59

63

Boot Hill

COVER

← *to Nevada City*

1. Smith and Boyd Livery Stable (Opera House)—1900
2. J. F. Stoer Saloon (Smith and Boyd Saloon/Bale of Hay Saloon)—1866
3. Mechanical Bakery Site—1863
4. Sauerbier Blacksmith Shop—1863
5. Frank Prasch Blacksmith Shop—1864
6. W. P. Armstrong Store (Montana Picture Gallery)—1863
7. S. R. Buford Store (Wells Fargo Coffee House, next door)—1875
8. McClurg and Ptorney Mercantile (Second Wells Fargo Office)—1863
9. Star Billiard Hall (E. L. Smith Store)—1863
10. Content Corner (Bob's Place)—1864
11. Stonewall Hall (Dudley Garage)—1864
12. Miner's Cafe (Virginia City Cafe)—1915

13. F. R. Merk Building (Pioneer Bar)—1866
14. Creighton Stone Block (Copper Palace)—1864
15. Allen and Millard Bank (Hussey, Dahler and Co. Bank)—1864
16. Old City Hall (Elks Club)—1897
17. Madison County Courthouse—1875–76
18. C. L. Dahler House (Pankey House)—1875
19. McKay/McNulty House—1864
20. Territorial Governor's Mansion (Benjamin F. Potts's House)—1864

21. Gohn House—1864
22. Virginia City Museum and Library (Thompson-Hickman Museum)—1918
23. Pace House—1935
24. Adobetown School (relocated)
25. Aunt Julia's (Kohl) House—1875
26. Dance and Stuart Store (reconstruction)
27. Kramer Building (Dress Shop)—1863
28. G. Goldberg Store (McGovern Dry Goods)—1863
29. Strasburger Colorado Store (Jewelry Store)—1863

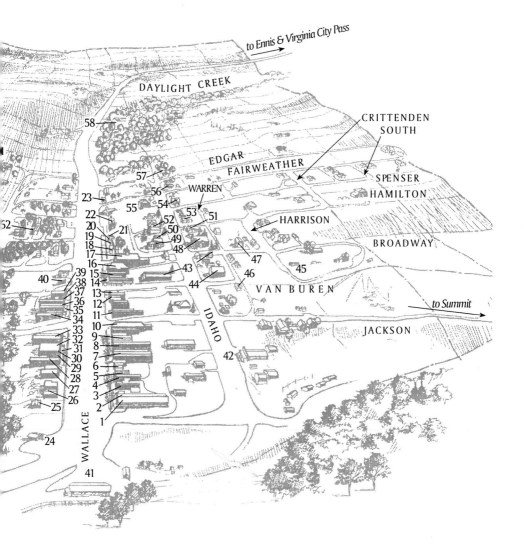

to Ennis & Virginia City Pass

DAYLIGHT CREEK

CRITTENDEN
SOUTH

58

EDGAR
FAIRWEATHER

57

SPENSER

56   WARREN

23   55   54

HAMILTON

22   52   53   51

20   50   HARRISON

19   21   49

18   48   BROADWAY

17

16   47

40   39   15   43   45

38   14   44   46

37   13   VAN BUREN

36   12

35   11   to Summit

34   10

33   9   JACKSON

32   8

31   7   42

30   6

29   5

28   4

27   3

26   2

25   1

24

WALLACE

41

52

Virginia City's population dropped drastically after gold was discovered in July 1864 in Last Chance Gulch and miners and their followers stampeded to Helena, the newest mining camp. By 1866, the year this photograph was taken from the west side of Alder Gulch looking up Wallace Street, an observer wrote: "Virginia looks like a large town minus the people."

Historic Overview

VIRGINIA CITY is "different from anything which I had ever before seen," Ellen Fletcher wrote to eastern friends in a letter describing her new home in southwestern Montana Territory. A gold-mining town in the upper Ruby River Valley where Daylight Creek flows into Alder Gulch, Virginia City sprawled along the foothills of the Tobacco Root Mountains; mountains that were bare and brown when Ellen and her husband Billy arrived in July 1866. "There isn't a tree in sight," Ellen wrote. "All have been cut down for wood, and all about the city, the ground is cut and dug up by the mining which is constantly going on."

Three years before the Fletchers followed other fortune hunters to Alder Gulch, gold had been discovered by six miners, led by Bill Fairweather and Henry Edgar, who had been prospecting near Bannack, seventy miles west of Alder Gulch. Disillusioned with dwindling returns from the Bannack fields, the men were on their way to the Yellowstone country when Crow Indians turned them back. Stopping on May 26, 1863, to prospect along a small creek, they panned enough gold to persuade them they had found rich diggings. Before returning to Bannack on May 30 for supplies, the men staked twelve claims, recorded water rights, and named the gulch Alder because of a "large fringe of Alder growing along the creek," Henry Edgar wrote in a reminiscence.

Once back in Bannack, news of their find spread fast, and when the six men left Bannack on June 2 to return to Alder Gulch, about two hundred miners followed them. Along the way the Fairweather party forced a halt and called a meeting to guarantee protection of their original twelve claims. On June 5 five of Fairweather's men slipped away and returned to Alder Gulch to secure their claims. The next day Edgar led the miners to the mouth of the gulch.

For several days stampeding men and pack animals fought through dense stands of alder along the gulch bottom. Within a week, according to N. P. Langford, an early settler, "hundreds of tents, brush wakeups, and rude log cabins" dotted the gulch in a haphazard manner, and the hills were denuded of trees. The makeshift lodgings barely sheltered the miners, who were "upheaving, sluicing, drifting, and cradling the inexhaustible bed of auriferous gravel," Langford wrote.

From those first days to the present, Virginia City and the surrounding countryside have been shaped and reshaped by people seeking livelihoods. Unlike many western mining towns that succumbed to depleted mineral deposits or were burned to the ground, Virginia City survived as a viable community. Buildings from the 1860s, when Virginia City thrived as a gold-mining town and territorial capital, still stand. Shops and residences built in the 1870s and 1880s during Virginia City's evolution into a regional marketing hub and seat of an expanding county government, serve similar functions today. Visitors walking Virginia City streets feel the presence of the early miners, traders, freighters, entertainers, business and civic leaders, and their families.

To go back beyond the 1860s, visitors must rely on imagination to "see" the gulch as it once was. Archaeological evidence of early native inhabitants was destroyed when miners churned the earth and washed a good portion of it away. Evidence elsewhere in the Missouri headwaters region suggests that people have occupied the area for at least twelve thousand years. Salish people lived in the Missouri headwater country before the 1600s. Piegans and Bloods of the Blackfeet Nation; as well as Crow, Shoshone, Snake, and Bannock peoples passed through the area on hunting and warring trips. Cree families frequently camped near Virginia City.

Reminders of this Native American heritage remain in written records. The Ruby River flowing west of the gulch, for example, was first listed on government maps as the "Passamari," a Snake Indian word variously translated as "the water of the cottonwood groves" and "quaking aspen grove." Today alder clumps are not as thick in the gulch as they were in 1863, but cottonwoods as well as quaking aspen still line the creek.

Many names in the area reflect the natural environment or the town founders' origins. While Alder Gulch drew its name from its western environment, Virginia City's name came from the East and is a reminder of the passions of opposing Union and Confederate sympathizers in the West during the Civil War. On June 9, 1863, just three days after Edgar and his followers stampeded the gulch, a group of men held a miners' meeting to organize the Fairweather Mining District and establish the governing structure for the camp in Alder Gulch. Dr. G. G. Bissell was elected judge of the miners' court. One week later, a group of land speculators filed with the miners' district a town site claim to 320 acres that the speculators intended to divide into lots and sell. The group named their company the Varina Town Company, for Confederate president Jefferson Davis's wife. Dr. Bissell, a staunch Union supporter, dropped Varina and wrote in Virginia on the official town site documents that, as judge of the miners' court, he was required to sign and file.

The miners' meeting that was called on June 9, as well as the informal meeting called by Fairweather's party during their return to the gulch a few days earlier, were common in mining camps. Mining strikes usually occurred in isolated areas removed from federal, territorial, or state authority. To provide some form of legal protection close at hand, miners usually held a miners' meeting soon after a strike to organize a mining district, elect officers, and set forth laws that provided a rudimentary system of justice for individuals but focused primarily on the protection of claims; description of claim locations; and regulations for working the claims, such as the volume of water that could be used at each mine site. Officials elected at a miners' meeting included a president to direct the district's business, a judge to preside over the miners' court, a sheriff, and a recorder to register all mining claim legal documents. Although mining districts and their laws were extralegal, they provided a rather loose form of democratic government to hold in check a community of independent and sometimes unruly residents until territorial officials organized governing structures for the mining site.

Among the first business addressed by the Fairweather Mining District following the miners' meeting in Alder Gulch was the processing of mining claims as well as the claim to the town site itself. Documents signed by mining district judge G. G. Bissell included the Virginia Town Company's original Virginia City town plat, which has since been lost. The town site's official plat, which is still in use, was drawn in 1868 and covers 579 acres divided into 274 blocks. The plat's street design is a traditional eastern grid of vertical and horizontal streets superimposed upon the hilly terrain.

Virginia City's vertical and horizontal street grid contrasts with the randomly wandering streets and paths of many western mining towns. Efforts to maintain the orderly pattern began as early as 1865, when the city council passed an ordinance stipulating that buildings encroaching on the town's streets would be torn down. An exception in the ordinance stated that "houses not in the middle of the street will not be disturbed."

In 1868 Virginia City applied for a federal patent, and city boundaries were resurveyed. Using the 1868 plat as a base, a new map was drawn in 1869 and attached to the application that records 569.75 acres within the town site. After the patent was issued on June 15, 1872, the city owned the land within the town and was authorized to sell unclaimed lots, bringing money into the municipal treasury rather than a real estate company's bank account.

When Virginia City was founded, western Montana was part of Idaho Territory, which had been created by the United States Congress in March 1863, following a gold rush to the Idaho region. By the time the Idaho territorial papers were filed, Idaho gold was running out, and news of the Alder Gulch strike immediately attracted miners leaving less lucrative camps in Idaho as well as in Colorado and California. Easterners, or people from "the states," began arriving in late 1863. By spring of 1864 nine mining camps dotted the gulch, which begins about fourteen miles west and slightly north of Virginia City, then curves south near Virginia City's western boundary.

Today's visitors can locate some of the early mining camps. On the south side of Montana Highway 287 west of Virginia City are a few remains of Central City, and on the north side of the highway across from the mining museum is a cluster of preserved gold rush buildings that are open to the public in Nevada City. Beyond Nevada City a highway marker indicates where Adobetown once stood. Driving south on Jackson Street out of Virginia City are the remains of a few

CITY OF VIRGINI[A]

MONTANA.

Established July 1863.

SURVEYED AND DRAWN BY J.L. CORBETT, CIVIL ENGINEE[R]

BY ORDER OF THE CITY COUNCIL

May 1868.

(PROPOSED) COURTHOUSE.

EPISCOPAL CHURCH.

Total Area 579¾ Acres.

When Virginia City applied for a federal town site patent in 1868, city officials commissioned John L. Corbett to draw the plat map reproduced on this page to accompany the application.

The map, which is still the legal plat of Virginia City, graphically portrays the town fathers' dreams. Details shown on the square grid of proposed streets include three city parks, three cemeteries, and agricultural areas or greenways named Fisher's Garden and Romeo's Garden that were set aside for vegetable gardens.

The three buildings on the plat's borders represent the town's perception of its political and civic future. The Masonic Temple building, portrayed in the upper right, had been completed in December 1867, but the drawings of the capitol and Episcopal church were merely artistic renderings. Neither the capitol nor the Episcopal church depicted on the map ever materialized, although a frame Episcopal church was built in 1868, and in 1902 the stone church in use today replaced the frame building. During Virginia City's reign as Montana's territorial capital from 1865 to 1875, official government offices were located in several buildings. Courtesy Montana Historical Society Library, Helena.

buildings in Summit. A stone mill built circa 1866 as part of an ore-processing facility remains in Union City, also south of Virginia City. The sites of Junction, Highland, and Pine Grove have blended back into the landscape.

Because of the highly mobile nature of many mining-area inhabitants, it is difficult to determine population figures for such regions. It is estimated, however, that by mid-1864 at least 10,000 people lived along the fourteen-mile gulch. Probably about 5,000 people lived within Virginia City at its peak. In the October 1864 election 2,300 residents voted, which number would not, of course, include women and children or franchised voters who failed to go to the polls. The town's 1868 application for a patent listed 2,500 residents, but the first census in 1870, taken after new gold strikes lured away residents, registered fewer than 900 people in Virginia City.

In western goldfields miners traditionally pursued with single-minded dedication their goal of making money as quickly as possible before moving on, leaving to others the business of providing goods, services, and entertainment, and of settling and developing the area. Almost as soon as the miners began working the gulch, traders moved into camp. "Men in Virginia City," F. E. W. Patten wrote in August 1863, "are more engaged in search[ing] for . . . gold than preparing for comfort, or for the approaching winter. . . . Many men are to be seen selling merchandise in tents, under bush arbors and in wagons."

The first permanent commercial building was a log cabin built in June 1863 to house a bakery. A saloon occupied the second commercial building. By mid to late summer the town included, among other businesses, a blacksmith's shop, brewery, hotel and eatery, and livery stable.

Among the early merchants in western mining towns were European Jews, many from Prussia, Bavaria, and Poland, who

ALDER GULCH
IN SOUTHWEST MONTANA

SCALE IN MILES

10   20   30

North

Holter Lake

Hauser Lake

Confederate Gulch

Helena ★

Canyon Ferry Lake

Area shown on larger map

15

90

Boulder

69

Butte

MISSOURI RIVER

Whitehall

Missouri
Headwaters

15

2

55

41

90

JEFFERSON RIVER

287

BIG HOLE RIVER

Tobacco Root Mts.

Norris

84

MADISON RIVER

Bozeman

Twin Bridges

Sheridan

287

41

Ruby
Junction
Adobetown
Nevada City
Central City

Ennis

Madison Range

Alder

Ruby Res.

Virginia City

Pine Grove
Highland
Summit

Union City

GALLATIN RIVER

Dillon

BEAVERHEAD RIVER

Ruby Range

RUBY RIVER

Alder Gulch

Snowcrest Range

Gravelly Range

MADISON RIVER

287

Bannack

Quake Lake

Hebgen
Lake

IDAHO

15

West Yellowstone

IDAHO

had immigrated to California during the 1848 gold rush. They sold their merchandise to California miners and eventually developed networks of family-owned dry-goods stores as they moved eastward with new gold strikes. At least eleven Jewish merchants owned Virginia City businesses. John and Moses Morris, for example, ran clothing stores in Denver, Virginia City, and Helena. Gumbert Goldberg, who joined his brother-in-law, John Morris, in the clothing business, held Passover seder services in his home for Jewish families until he left Virginia City in 1866. Solomon Content built Virginia City's most prestigious commercial building in 1864.

Investors and speculators in mining claims and real estate appeared nearly as quickly as merchants. Road agents were in the region from the outset as well, and they traveled the road between Bannack and Virginia City robbing stage coaches and other travelers with little interference from the miners' court and none from the territorial legal system. Following a particularly senseless killing in December 1863, community leaders organized vigilance committees in Nevada City and Virginia City. From late December 1863 until early March 1864, the vigilantes hung at least twenty-four men, tracking some suspects across southwestern Montana before capturing them and hanging them on the spot. The vigilantes accused Henry Plummer, who served as sheriff in Bannack and Virginia City, of directing the bandits. Surprising Plummer and two of his associates in Bannack on January 10, the vigilantes hanged the three men immediately without benefit of trials.

The number of violent crimes dropped dramatically after the vigilante campaign against Plummer's gang ended in March. Within two months vigilante justice and the mining district committee were replaced by a more responsive territorial government when Congress separated western Montana

The original Gothic arches that graced the Nowlan and Weary Bank (**site 39**) when it was built in 1864 are shown in this photograph taken two years later. During a 1910 remodeling, the arches were removed, and stucco, scored to look like brick, covered the original stone facade. Greek Revival pilasters as well as fanlights trimmed the building next door (no longer standing) that was used by acting Governor Thomas Meagher for his executive office in 1866.

from Idaho Territory and created Montana Territory on May 26, 1864. Bannack was selected for the territorial capital, and Virginia City became seat of Madison County government. A frame building housed county offices until 1876 when a two-story brick courthouse was built. With Virginia City's ascendancy over Bannack, the first territorial legislature moved the capital to Virginia City on February 7, 1865. Without an official building, territorial government activities took place in rented rooms throughout the town.

Virginia City, the leading community in Alder Gulch, was the hub of a transportation network that connected the mining camps with distant towns and supply points. Several local stage lines carried passengers, mail, and gold before Wells, Fargo and Company became the dominant carrier after 1866. Two of the most heavily used supply sites were Fort Benton, Montana, a Missouri River destination port 235 miles north of Alder Gulch, and Salt Lake City, Utah, almost 500 miles south over the Corrinne–Virginia City Road. The long string of freighters that brought raw materials and finished products as well as food were significant to the mining district's survival. Unlike the agricultural frontier, where the first settlers raised their own food and sustained themselves in rural settings until towns developed later, the western mining frontier was urban from the beginning. Food as well as other products were freighted in until ranchers and farmers arrived and began to raise meat and produce for the growing towns.

Contrary to stereotype, mining towns attracted well-educated people, who brought with them expectations that the cultural and social pleasures they had enjoyed in the East would be part of their new lives. Fraternal lodges, civic institutions, and cultural clubs brought people together to discuss civic improvements and share common interests. In Virginia City, for example, many of the town's first business and professional men were Masons, who formed Montana's first Masonic Lodge in Virginia City on February 14, 1864.

By the summer of 1864 shoppers could buy milled lumber and quarry stone, groceries, dry goods, books, stationery, shoes, clothing, mining tools, and a copy of Virginia City's own newspaper, the *Montana Post*. Children attended subscription schools in Nevada City and Virginia City. Saloons, dance halls, and brothels prospered. DeWitt Waugh, local band director, organized the Montana Theatre in September 1864 and rented a performance hall. Catholic church services had been held

Residents in isolated mining camps depended on freighters for nearly all daily necessities before local farmers, ranchers, and craftsmen began growing food and supplying finished products. Among the many trans-portation entrepreneurs hauling goods to Virginia City were the freighters who posed on Van Buren Street for this circa 1866 photograph.

since November 1863. Baptist and Methodist ministers came to town in 1864, and the Methodists built the first church that December. Many of the same men who formed the vigilantes and the Masonic Lodge organized the Montana Historical Society in February 1865, suggesting their awareness of the historical significance of Virginia City and its people.

Men far outnumbered women during Virginia City's early days. Henry N. Blake remembered attending a dance shortly after his arrival where "there were twelve women and fifty men. There were no wallflowers," he wrote, "and the women had no rest during the festivities." Blake, a young

Boston attorney who came to Alder Gulch in 1866, was editor of both the *Montana Post* and the *Montanian* in Virginia City before returning to the practice of law. He moved to Helena in 1889 to become the Montana Supreme Court's first chief justice.

Many of the first women in town were dancers in the hurdy-gurdy houses where one dance sold for a dollar in gold dust. Not all were single women. Some women, married to miners down on their luck, worked at the dance halls to support their families. A few of the dancers supplemented their income as prostitutes. As more women and children arrived, dress balls, dances, and family social gatherings became common. In a letter to his wife, Episcopal Bishop Daniel Tuttle, who arrived in 1867, wrote, "kind hearts are here, cultivated women are here, intelligent society is here."

Virginia City's children had few textbooks at first, but opportunities to learn existed from the beginning. Thomas Dimsdale, an Englishman who came to Virginia City in June 1863, tutored children in his home for a fee until he was hired as editor of the *Montana Post*. While he was editor he wrote *The Vigilantes of Montana*, the first book published in Montana. Children attended subscription schools until 1866 when the first Montana territorial legislature authorized counties to levy property taxes to pay for a public education system. Governor Sidney Edgerton appointed Dimsdale the first superintendent of schools, but Dimsdale died shortly after taking office. At its next session, the legislature made the position elective. Montana's first public school met in March 1866 in a Virginia City church, and in the fall of 1866 a log schoolhouse was built.

Despite brisk business opportunities and social, cultural, and educational amenities, life in Virginia City could be difficult. The area's isolation, a scarcity of nutritious foods and

Schools, churches, and other institutions signal the transition from transient mining camp to permanent community. Virginia City's first public school, Montana School District 1, opened in March 1866 in the former Baptist Union Church. That fall the log schoolhouse pictured above, circa 1867, was built on the southeast corner of Broadway and Warren streets, the present-day site of the J. E. Callaway house (**site 47**).

consumer goods, harsh weather, and economic uncertainties weighed heavily on residents.

Virginia City reached its peak as a mining community in 1865 and 1866. Even as civic groups organized; substantial buildings replaced log cabins; and fraternal organizations, literary societies, theater groups, churches, and schools appeared, the discovery of new goldfields in western Montana foretold Virginia City's approaching decline. On July 14, 1864, gold was discovered in Last Chance Gulch, 125 miles north of Alder Gulch, and the town of Helena was founded. Later that summer another strike was made in Confederate Gulch, east of Helena. The 1870 census shows 867 residents in Virginia City. Five years later voters dashed Virginia City's dreams and moved the capital to Helena.

At the end of the 1870s nearly one-third of Virginia City's

From 1865 to 1875, when Virginia ❧ clothing store in the building when
City was Montana's territorial this photograph was taken circa
capital, the territorial legislature 1882. Lewis Dudley removed the
met on the second floor of original stone front and replaced it
Stonewall Hall **(site 11)** built in 1864 with brick in 1914 to accommodate
on Wallace Street next to the Pony a garage. In 1925 Dudley tore down
Saloon on the corner of Jackson the Pony Saloon to enlarge his
Street. Richard O. Hickman ran a garage.

population were Chinese, segregated at the far west end of
Wallace Street by a city ordinance. According to the *Montana
Post,* the first Chinese came to Virginia City in June 1865. By
the end of 1866 it is estimated that about 150 Chinese lived in
the area. Many of the first Chinese to arrive were experienced
miners who had left played-out mining districts in California, the
Pacific Northwest, and Idaho. Following a pattern established in
earlier mining regions, when Euramericans left for richer strikes
elsewhere, the Chinese took over their mining claims and
reworked the diggings for another twenty-five years. Some
Chinese miners worked their claims alone, while others mined

in partnerships. J. Ross Browne, a federal mine observer, estimated that because of careless mining techniques only about half the gold in Alder Gulch had been taken out by 1868. The Chinese, denied access to richer claims, painstakingly extracted what earlier miners left behind.

Many Chinese in Virginia City were employed as domestic servants or were in restaurant and laundry businesses. Bishop Tuttle wrote in July 1867 that "Chinamen do nearly all the laundry work, and do it neatly too. Chinese servants are quite in vogue." Like their white counterparts, Chinese residents managed stores, owned brothels and gambling houses, and built their own Chinese temple, or joss house, and Masonic Lodge, neither of which still stands. Two hundred sixty-five Chinese lived in the gulch in 1880. By the turn of the century their numbers were dwindling, and no Chinese lived there after 1920.

Many African Americans, attracted by the goldfields, came west, especially after the Civil War. Although not as well documented as were the Chinese, early writings about Virginia City refer to blacks in the region, and an African American Pioneer Social Club formed in Alder Gulch in 1867. Henry N. Blake noted in his memoirs that thirty African Americans lived in Virginia City in 1866. Until her death in 1939, Sarah Bickford, a black woman, owned and managed the Virginia City Water Company, which she inherited from her white husband upon his death in 1900.

By 1880 only about 634 people lived in Virginia City. During the next decade the town's economy and population benefited from increased demand and higher prices for silver as well as from technological advances in gold-mining techniques and from railroad construction in the territory. The Conrey Placer Mining Company, with headquarters in Boston, Massachusetts, an office in Virginia City, and employee housing in Ruby, west

In April 1875 Virginia City, smarting over its loss of the territorial capital to Helena, elected to build a county courthouse to salve its wounds (**site 17**). Designed by Loren B. Olds, Virginia City's best-known architect, the building, shown here in an early undated photograph, was completed in 1876 at the height of Italianate architecture's popularity in the United States. The corner pilasters, second-story balcony, interior side chimneys, roof brackets, and cupola are characteristics of Italianate style.

of Virginia City, ran dredging operations in Alder Gulch from 1898 until 1922.

No railroad ever came into Virginia City. The town did respond, however, to indirect economic energy generated by construction activity and somewhat improved transportation opportunities after the Union Pacific Railroad's Utah and Northern line reached Butte in 1881. Under pressure from the Conrey Placer Company, the Northern Pacific Railroad ran a feeder line in 1901 to Alder, Virginia City's closest railhead nine miles to the west. The Humphreys Gold Production Company of Denver, Colorado, ran dryland dredges in the gulch from 1935 to 1937. While one last dryland dredging effort in 1940–41 ended the sporadic mining booms and boomlets in Alder Gulch, Virginia City remained a regional market and service center for local families well into the twentieth century.

The 1940s were Virginia City's bleakest years. Its population plummeted as men and women left to join the armed forces or to work in war-related industries during World War II. In 1941, when precious metal mining was deemed a non-essential industry for the war effort and Congress issued the Gold Mine Closing Order, only 380 people lived in the town. During the 1940s county business, a few local merchants, and an occasional tourist barely sustained Virginia City.

Virginia City's contemporary history began in the mid-1940s, when Charles and Sue Bovey, entranced by the town, inaugurated one of the first privately financed preservation programs in the West. The Boveys were wealthy Great Falls–area ranchers who passionately pursued Montana history through books and trips across the state, purchasing artifacts and buildings as well as nurturing statewide interest in preserving evidence of Montana's beginnings. In addition to the couple's preservation efforts, Charles Bovey also served in the Montana legislature first as a representative and then as a senator from 1942 to 1966.

In 1945 Bovey bought a Virginia City house built in 1868. For the next thirty-three years, until Charles Bovey's death in 1978, the couple bought buildings, paid for and supervised preservation efforts, and fostered tourism in Virginia City. In great part because of their efforts, today's visitors to Alder Gulch experience a slice of life in an early Montana mining town.

Over time, however, the mining town and especially the landscape have changed. Early hand placer mining rearranged the land through Alder Gulch, and hydraulicking washed down chunks of mountainside. Dredging introduced mass production to gold mining in the late nineteenth century, greatly increasing the amount of gold retrieved and changing forever the contours of the earth. Dredging literally turned the ground inside out, obliterating not only evidence of earlier native peoples but of the first mine and camp sites in the gulch, leaving behind a residue of uprooted trees and shrubs, dredge ponds, and serpentine-shaped rock piles lying atop the land like giant dragons.

Such is the heritage of mining towns across the West, and configuration of the land is as telling a mark of Virginia City's history as the rough log cabins built in 1863, the substantial stone and brick commercial buildings that replaced the modest cabins, and the Victorian homes that successful businessmen continued to build until the end of the century.

Today Virginia City is a blend of old and new. One hundred and thirty-five years after the gold strike in Alder Gulch Virginia City carries on its business along the same streets and in the same structures that served the early miners and settlers. New, rebuilt, and remodeled homes and businesses are evident as well. To appreciate this living history setting, visitors need to search for clues imprinted on buildings and landscape that tell the story of Virginia City, past and present.

Buildings and Landscape
Tell Virginia City's Story

✛⟨══⟩✛

Blessed by good fortune, many of Virginia City's buildings constructed between 1863 and the late 1870s appear today much as they did then. No catastrophic fire burned out the town, and the region's dry climate discouraged damage from rot and insects and saved roofs from collapsing under weighty snowfalls. Local people as well as "outsiders" such as Sue and Charles Bovey preserved buildings and artifacts and persevered in their efforts to establish the town as a historic site. Because of the Boveys' efforts, Virginia City was designated a National Historic Landmark in 1961. The National Historic Registration Act, passed by Congress in 1966, created the National Register of Historic Places, and in 1976 Virginia City was listed on the Register.

Like other mining communities, Virginia City's character was set by its early inhabitants. Gold brought miners to the region in May 1863, and miners' gold lured investors, speculators, and entrepreneurs. Although many of the people who built the first crude shelters and shops left before winter set in, those who remained were soon joined by others. This core group of miners and businessmen set the direction of Virginia City's development as a regional transportation and trading hub. By the end of the town's second year, other new residents, many from the East, arrived, bringing with them cultural and social customs as well as architectural styles already established in eastern communities.

Similar periods of development in other western mining towns have been referred to as the settlement phase, camp phase, and town phase. During the settlement phase, described as the moment of discovery and the earliest days of the boom, miners lived in tents or built crude, temporary shelters as they concentrated on their search for gold. During the camp phase, miners and the merchants who followed constructed more permanent buildings out of available materials but paid little attention to style. Buildings constructed during the town phase reflected the architectural fashions of the day and used more imported or manufactured material.

Western mining towns had existed for more than a dozen years by the time of the Alder Gulch strike. From its beginning settlement phase, Virginia City benefited from a mining network that began in California in 1848 and moved east as new goldfields were discovered in Colorado and Idaho. Experienced miners quickly learned of new strikes; traders knew what goods and services were needed, how to get them to new locations, and how to set up shop as soon as they arrived on the scene. Building necessities, such as planed lumber and construction tools, were freighted in from Bannack. Sawmills, for example, probably were working in the gulch by mid-June 1863. Carpenters came to the gulch shortly after the strike, and they brought their skills with them.

Virginia City's progression, in less than two years, through the three stages of development, occurred so quickly that each successive phase telescoped one into another. Layered remnants of each phase are evident in the buildings that remain

During the summer of 1863 Virginia Citians sought social companionship in the small, V-notched log dance hall that still stands within the Sauerbier Blacksmith Shop (site 4). By 1944 when the above photograph was taken, tall French doors and a few pieces of molding trim on the facade were the only reminders of the building's past elegance.

today. Many structures display more than one architectural style, for example, or show the effects of having been remodeled, added to, and modified in a variety of ways to take advantage of improved construction materials and techniques or to accommodate changing needs. Such alterations bear witness to the town's unfolding history.

The Sauerbier Blacksmith Shop (site 4), for example, exemplifies the layering effect of Virginia City's development. The structure began as a small log cabin built in June 1863. Later that fall, the cabin was incorporated into a larger frame building, and it assumed the appearance of a typical 1860s Virginia City storefront with the additions of a western style false front and two pairs of double French doors topped by a six-light transom (a row of windows above the doors) and a wooden cornice ornamented with dentils (small, projecting rectangular blocks). By 1878 the Sauerbier building had been converted to a blacksmith shop. One pair of French doors had been removed and a wider door installed to accommodate wagons and buggies. Several sheds were attached to the west and south walls of the shop during the next twenty years, and the building looks today much as it did in 1904. After he bought the building in 1947, C. A. Bovey stabilized and carefully repaired the badly weathered false front while maintaining its aged appearance.

Architectural and construction features, such as those seen on the Sauerbier Blacksmith Shop, are cultural records that document community histories as well as building styles and changes over time. Such tangible records help to explain when towns developed, what kind of people settled them, where they came from, and what inhabitants did to sustain themselves and their communities. Virginia City architecture mirrored, within local limitations, building styles common in the East during the nineteenth century, which was an age of architectural revivals in this country as well as in Europe. The first styles to reappear were classical Greek and Roman forms, followed by Gothic, Italianate, Renaissance, and other styles from earlier centuries.

Suggestions of several nineteenth-century architectural revival styles are seen in Virginia City, but the three most prevalent styles recognizable in structures built between 1863 and the late 1870s are Greek Revival, Gothic Revival, and Italianate, often subdued and modified to accommodate available materials. Decorative features of Victorian architectural styles, such as Queen Anne, that became popular later in the century, were added to several of the early buildings,

The Montana Picture Gallery (site 6), built in 1863 and shown here in the late 1980s, is a classic western representation of Greek Revival with a central door flanked by pilasters and two large multipaned windows. The building's false front is strictly western vernacular. Courtesy State Historic Preservation Office, Helena.

particularly residences, when they were remodeled in the 1880s and 1890s.

Greek Revival buildings in America's West usually were rectangular with the short side facing front. Identifying features include pilasters (flat rectangular strips that look like flattened columns attached to a wall) to simulate the classic columns of Greek temples, central doorways and windows delineated with triangular pediments (triangular beams of wood or masonry placed over doors and windows), and formal casings at window openings. Gothic Revival buildings are recognizable by steeply pitched roofs; bargeboard trim along roof edges; pointed-arch, high dormer windows; elaborate board-and-batten siding covering front sections; and battlements (calling to mind the parapets that protected roof edges of medieval European castles) along the roofline.

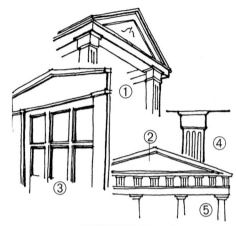

Typical Greek Revival Details
1. Portico (Porch)
2. Triangular Pediment
3. Formal Casings at Window Openings
4. Pilasters (columns engaged in walls)
5. Columns

DRAWINGS BY KEN SIEVERT, GREAT FALLS

By the 1860s the popularity of Greek Revival and Gothic Revival was waning in the East. Few examples of either style exist in the state outside Virginia City, which developed at the end of the styles' eastern popularity and at the beginning of Montana's settlement.

Italianate buildings, which began to appear in the West in the 1870s, were popular from about 1840 to 1885 in the East. Distinguishing Italianate details are low-hipped roofs, sloping inward on all four sides and flat in appearance; large supporting brackets under eaves; tall windows, often with hoods or heavy projecting trim; quoins (projecting stones on the corners, frequently exaggerated in size); and square or rectangular towers, especially on public buildings.

Although architectural styles are expressed differently in residential, commercial, and public buildings, each style's distinctive elements are recognizable and are the kind of clues to look for in identifying and dating Virginia City buildings. The following commercial, government, ecclesiastical, and residential structures built during Virginia City's three developmental phases were selected because their architectural features are

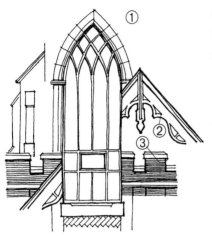

Gothic Revival Elements

① Pointed arches and openings

② "Gingerbread" verge or bargeboard (called a fascia in today's construction vocabulary)

③ Battlements at the tops of walls (used for defense during medieval times)

Italianate Features

① Large brackets along cornice (sometimes in pairs)

② Tall windows with "hoods" or "labeled moldings" (heavy projecting trims)

③ Rusticated quoins (projecting corner stones—often of an exaggerated size)

④ Wide overhangs

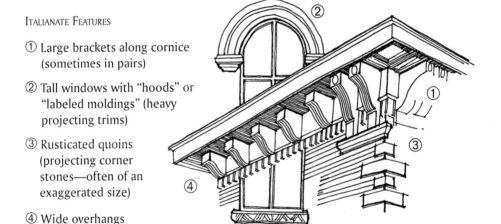

easily recognizable. Each selection is intended to direct discerning eyes and inquisitive minds to similar features at other sites. Because more than one feature representing different architectural styles frequently appear on the same building, some sites are referred to more than once.

Site numbers in parenthesis refer to the map on pages 4 and 5. The buildings are listed numerically beginning at the west end of Wallace Street.

SETTLEMENT PHASE

As with other mining strikes, the first miners in Alder Gulch lived on their claims in tents, under wagon beds, in dugouts, under sheltering rocks, or in huts. Such shelters disappeared as quickly as they had appeared. Virginia City's next buildings were crude log cabins, many along Jackson Street leading to mine claims south of town. Most of these, too, are gone now, but a few, such as the tiny log cabin enclosed within the Sauerbier Blacksmith Shop (site 4), remain. By fall 1863 commercial building was shifting to Wallace Street.

CAMP PHASE

Virginia City's settlement and camp phases blended together that first summer. Vernacular western buildings, that is, structures built by craftsmen who adhered to local, in this case, western tradition, typify camp phase architecture. Speed, rather than style, was the builder's driving force. Early camp phase buildings often are hard to distinguish from those built during the settlement phase. An example is the Kramer building or dress shop (site 27). Round logs, crudely notched together at the corners, were covered with a roof of round poles and dirt. The original dirt-covered pole roof is barely visible along the west side poking out from beneath the present roof. Board-and-batten siding later covered the front and sides, hiding most of the logs.

Although stone buildings frequently are pointed to as examples of the kind of substantial structures that epitomize the town phase of development, Virginia City's first stone building, Kiskadden's Stone Block (site 32), was constructed during the town's first summer. Rubble stones gathered in the area were hauled to the site and placed in their rough state from ground level to just above the doors. The stones were then

From 1865 to 1875 territorial government offices occupied the second floor above various first-floor retail stores, including Armstrong and Johnson in Content Corner, Virginia City's premier commercial building, pictured above circa 1875 (**site 10**). In the turn-of-the-century photograph below, the original rubble stone covered with scored stucco has been replaced by a brick front, and display windows have replaced the Gothic arches. On the east side, original arched windows remain. Scored stucco still covers part of the back section of the east wall but has worn away on the front of the east wall revealing the rubble stone.

The J. B. LaBeau Jewelry Store, shown above, was photographed sometime after 1948, when Charles Bovey added a porch to protect the classic Greek Revival facade (**site 30**). Board and batten, clapboard, and wide drop siding, the three most frequently used board sidings in Virginia City, are all evident on the building, now a toy store. Courtesy State Historic Preservation Office, Helena. Below, left to right, the LaBeau Jewelry, J. Oliver's City Bakery, Kiskadden's Stone Block (a livery stable after 1871), and the Anaconda Hotel (now the Fairweather Inn) were photographed circa 1936 before the Bovey restorations (**sites 30–33**).

When this photograph was taken circa 1866, Kiskadden's Stone Block (site 32) housed three stores on the first floor beneath a second-floor meeting hall. The original scored stucco covers the rubble stone front, and the two large doors of the center store are still in their original setting. One of the center doors was installed between the two windows on the second floor when the sliding livery door, seen in the photograph on the opposite page, was added in 1871.

covered with stucco, which was scored to give the appearance of smooth, rectangular cut stones. This technique, common in both the East and the West, was used with cut quarry stone as well as rubble stone. Other examples of stuccoed stone buildings in Virginia City include Content Corner (site 10) and the Methodist Church (site 44).

A sawmill was operating in the gulch just west of Virginia City by July 1863, and by the following summer several sawmills were producing a variety of boards for exterior finish work. Most common in Virginia City during this period were board and batten, clapboard, and drop siding. Board and batten, also used for roofs, consists of wide, usually 1-inch by 12-inch boards, rough sawn, nailed on vertically, with the cracks covered with a narrow strip, about ½ inch by 3 inches. Clapboards are horizontal boards about ½ inch by 6 inches, usually planed, each overlapping the top edge of the one below. Drop siding, which came in the late 1860s, is horizontal siding planed from a board approximately 1 inch by 8 inches, with a tongue-and-groove edge. All three styles of boards are seen on the J. B. LaBeau or toy store (site 30). Board and batten covers the porch roof, clapboard covers the false front, and wide drop siding was added later to the sides and back. Siding frequently was placed over logs to hide the rough construction.

When structures were built wall to wall, as many of Virginia City's commercial buildings were, boards were applied only to visible portions such as fronts or along one side if the building stood on a corner. By looking carefully, perhaps at a building next to a vacant lot, visitors can see exposed log walls that once were hidden by another structure, such as the east wall of the Bale of Hay Saloon (site 2), next to the now empty site where the Mechanical Bakery once stood (site 3).

One of the most familiar characteristics of western towns are false board fronts, which create the illusion of taller buildings. False fronts are seen on Kiskadden's Stone Block (site 32), the Greek Revival–style frame McClurg and Ptorney Mercantile (site 8), and the Strasburger Colorado Store (site 29), all built in 1863. False fronts are also found on later buildings such as the Bale of Hay Saloon (site 2) and the Bonanza Inn (site 42), both built in 1866, well into Virginia City's town phase. Bay windows, as in the Star Billiard Hall (site 9), also were installed during the camp phase. The Renaissance Revival–inspired storefront on the Strasburger Store (site 29) was considered innovative in the 1860s. Not until the 1880s did the store's reverse bay–style door and window become standard for store facades.

Entrances to commercial buildings during Virginia City's first years frequently had two or three sets of French doors

False fronts make structures look ✧ Hay Saloon) and the log building next
more imposing as demonstrated by to it, which housed the Mechanical
this 1870s photograph of the log Bakery, Virginia City's first commercial
J. F. Stoer liquor store (later Smith structure built in June 1863 (sites 2
and Boyd Saloon and now the Bale of and 3).

that let in fresh air and sunshine during warm weather and
light during the winter months. Early glass window panes,
freighted in from Salt Lake City or Fort Benton, were expensive
and small. Each pane measured six inches by eight inches and
cost about one dollar. The small size of the panes made them
easier to pack and less likely to break on the jarring overland
trip. Many original window panes have been broken, but those
remaining are easily recognized by imperfections such as pits,
shimmers, or ridges in the glass, noticeable, for instance, in
the Strasburger Store (site 29).

Residences, like commercial structures built during Virginia
City's camp phase, were plain, western vernacular buildings,
put together quickly using easily obtained materials. Usually
one story, the log or frame homes were simple rectangles or ell-
shapes with gable roofs. Homes like Mrs. Slade's house (site 46)
are representative of Virginia City's camp phase residences.

Pediments over windows and door and bracketed wood cornices at the roofline distinguish the 1864 Allen and Millard Bank (later Hall and Bennett), Montana Territory's first financial institution to offer full banking services, including authority to write drafts on a New York bank (**site 15**). Photograph circa 1890.

TOWN PHASE

During 1864, the year Montana Territory was created, more substantial and sophisticated buildings, displaying their owners' wealth and confidence in the town's future, signaled Virginia City's passage into the town phase of development. Just as the settlement and camp phases blended together, so did the camp phase overlap the beginning of the town phase. Structures such as the Hangman's building (site 40) built early in the year, for example, epitomize

Hints of popular architectural styles such as the Gothic Revival scalloped bargeboards and Greek Revival pedimented windows shown in this undated photograph of the McKay/McNulty house, are common features of many early Virginia City homes. The home's center section, built circa 1870, connects two small log cabins built in 1864 (**site 19**).

unpretentious vernacular styles. Residences like the Potts's house (**site 20**) and the McKay/McNulty house (**site 19**) built in 1864, differ little from homes built in late 1863. The otherwise plain fronts on houses built during this period often were relieved by bargeboards (gingerbread trim cut in a linear or curved pattern) such as the trim along the gables of the Potts's house.

The town's growing wealth and sophistication, however, are evident in buildings erected a few months later in the year such as the Allen and Millard Bank (**site 15**) that features Greek Revival pediments above the door and window openings. Elements of Gothic architecture also are evident on Virginia City's 1864 buildings. Content Corner (**site 10**), built of stone, was Virginia City's most prestigious commercial building. The

Battlements along the roofline and arched designs on the walls of the *Montana Post* building (site 34), as well as arched windows in the stone print shop behind the newspaper office, typify Carpenter Gothic, a vernacular version of the Gothic Revival style. Photograph circa 1866.

original Gothic front was replaced with a plate glass storefront in 1895, but Gothic transoms on the balcony doors remain, as do the Gothic pointed arches along the side of the building. Gothic pointed arches also are evident on the stone print shop, which was added to the back of the *Montana Post* building in 1865 (site 34). Board-and-batten siding covers the front of the *Post* and battlements run along the roofline.

Joseph Griffith and William Thompson, who ran a sawmill and lumberyard in Virginia City, opened the first quarry in the gulch by July 1864 to supply cut stones. The Creighton Stone Block (site 14) was the first Virginia City structure built of quarry stone. Round-topped, semicircular arched openings suggest Romanesque style, reflecting classical Roman design.

Virginia City's Masonic Lodge, Montana Territory's first fraternal organization, met above Paris Pfouts Store, shown in this circa 1869 photograph, from 1865 until the Mason's own building, to the right of Pfouts Store, was completed in 1867 (**sites 37** and **38**). Masons still meet in the beautifully preserved ashlar stone–front building.

Recessed French doors are topped by transom fanlights, semicircular windows with mullion bars (thin strips of wood) radiating over the glass like a fan.

In 1867 a new Masonic Temple (**site 38**) was built to accommodate the increasing activities of Masonic members. Several stores occupied the first floor until 1916. The United States Post Office has occupied the space since then. The ashlar stone–front (square cut stone) building features simplified Renaissance Revival elements, characterized by quoins (stones that mark the corners). The building looks today exactly as it did in 1867.

On July 4, 1867, Wilbur Fisk and Harriet Fenn Sanders moved into the Carpenter Gothic cottage shown behind the George E. Gohn house in the pen and ink drawing above (**sites 51** and **21**). The steeply pitched gable in the upper center facade of the Sanders home is a typical Gothic Revival application. The 1899 photograph, below, shows the addition of a Queen Anne–style porch to the right side of the house. Drawing from M. A. Leeson, *History of Montana, 1739–1885* (Chicago: Warner, Beers and Co., 1885), 771.

J. E. Callaway built this house in 1876, at (site 47). The gracious home, shown
the end of Virginia City's glory days, as in a 1946 photograph, mixes elegant
a fitting tribute to his importance as a 1870s modified Italianate detailing with
territorial attorney and political leader intricate Gothic Revival bargeboards.

Wilbur Fisk Sanders, an attorney who came to Montana
in June 1863 and eventually became one of Montana's first
two United States senators, built a Carpenter Gothic home in
1867 (site 51). Carpenter Gothic homes became popular after
jigsaws were perfected, which made possible the intricate
porch trim. The elegant Sanders residence is an example of a
house built to proclaim its owner's wealth and rising status in
the community. Victorian Queen Anne features added in later
remodelings include the porch on the home's west side.

New building slowed in Virginia City during the 1870s,
1880s, and 1890s, although Victorian elements were imposed
on earlier buildings during remodeling that continued into the
twentieth century. One example of the changing styles is the C.
L. Dahler (Pankey) house (site 18). Built in 1875, this splendid

Built in 1875 and occupied by C. L. Dahler in 1884, the home pictured above was high-fashion Gothic Revival with its steeply pitched roof, tall central gable, and vertical board-and-batten siding (site 18). In the late 1890s Victorian-era bay windows, rear gable, and gingerbread decorating the front facade were added, giving the home the asymmetrical configuration of the Queen Anne style, as shown below. The front porch was rebuilt in 1974. Both photographs are undated.

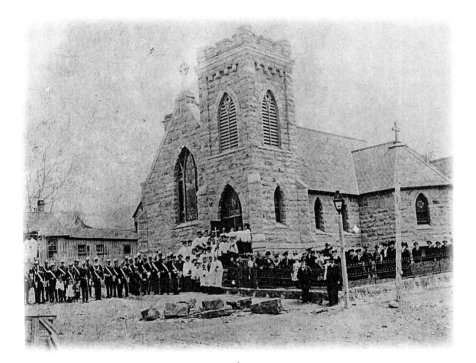

Parishioners and members of the Knights Templars, a Freemasonry order, pose in front of St. Paul's Episcopal Church at the 1904 dedication of the English Gothic–style building erected in 1902 (**site 48**). The congregation tore down the 1868 frame church on the site to make room for the native porphyry stone structure. Tiffany stained glass windows are encased in the Gothic arches.

Gothic Revival home is recognizable by its steeply pitched roof and tall front dormer. During the 1890s the residence was remodeled to reflect changing fashion. The added dormers and bay windows typify the asymmetrical configuration popular in Victorian Queen Anne residences.

Gothic Revival features such as tall pointed windows are evident on the Methodist Church (**site 44**) built in 1875, as well as St. Paul's Episcopal Church (**site 48**), one of Virginia City's last stylistically imposing buildings, built in 1902. A classic

Unlike most Gothic Revival homes, which usually were built of wood, this home, shown here in an undated photograph, was built of stone in 1884 by Virginia City businessman George Thexton (**site 54**).

example of residential Gothic Revival is the stone Thexton house (**site 54**). Its steeply pitched roof, pointed arch windows, and decorated brackets straddling the porch supports look very much today as they did when the house was built in 1884.

Distinguishing features of the Italianate style, which became popular in the 1870s, are evident in the brackets beneath the eaves, the low-pitched hip roof, and brackets on the tower of the brick Madison County Courthouse built in 1875 (**site 17**, photograph page 24). A cast iron storefront, popular commercial building ornamentation during the Italianate period, covers the front of the Metropolitan Meat Market (**site 36**), built in the late 1880s.

Standing amidst Virginia City's preserved buildings are structures built recently to duplicate original buildings that

Gothic arches, medallions, and building next door. Both buildings battlement motif on the original in this circa 1900 photograph are Dance and Stuart Store contrast gone, and a replica of the Dance with Greek Revival–style pediments and Stuart Store stands on the site above the window and door of the (site 26).

were torn down. An example is the Dance and Stuart Store (site 26), built of vintage logs by Charles Bovey in 1950 to replicate the original store demolished in 1925. Other structures, modified over time, are mixtures of old and new. The Fairweather Inn (site 33), for example, reflects eighty-three years of modifications.

The oldest section of the inn was built in 1863 as a one-story restaurant with a false front. A wood-framed storefront was installed in the 1880s with large plate glass windows and wood columns imitating cast iron. In 1896 it became the Anaconda Hotel. The Humphrey's Gold Corporation bought the building in 1935 and built a dormitory on the east side for its workers. When Humphrey dredges left the gulch in 1940, the building was abandoned. Charles Bovey bought the old hotel in 1946, adding a second story and a new facade that duplicates and uses some pieces from the Goodrich House, a

The deteriorating Anaconda Hotel is and buildings to its right attest to pictured here about 1916 before the popularity of false fronts with its restoration as part of the Fair-bracketed cornices and fanlights in weather Inn (**site 33**). The hotel Virginia City architecture.

hotel built in Bannack prior to the Alder Gulch gold run and later demolished. A dredge ladder that Bovey salvaged to use as a fire escape from the second story represents a later mining era. Bovey named the remodeled building Fairweather Inn to honor the man who discovered gold in the gulch. Although far different from the simple 1863 restaurant that is preserved within its walls, the various pieces that were combined to create today's Fairweather Inn span Montana's gold mining days from 1863 to 1935.

Smith and Boyd's Saloon and the false-fronted rubble stone Smith and Boyd Livery Stable appear to be thriving in the turn-of-the-century photograph above (sites 1 and 2). The saloon is now the Bale of Hay Saloon, and the livery, pictured below in the late 1980s, is the Opera House, home to Montana's oldest professional acting company, the Virginia City Players. In 1949 additions were added to the rear of the building, and a columned porch from the Morgan Evans mansion near Anaconda transformed the front of the old livery shown below after the remodeling. Opera House photograph courtesy State Historic Preservation Office, Helena.

The most basic placer mining technique requires only a pick and shovel to dig the sand and gravel and a pie plate–shaped pan to separate the gold from the gravel. Using these simple tools, two miners pan gold near Virginia City in this undated photograph.

MINING SITES

For fifty years the search for gold sculpted the countryside around Virginia City into a variety of shapes as mining technology became more sophisticated. Whether sinking shafts into the ground or scraping and washing away the earth's surface, mining forever changed the land's surface.

Gold comes from the earth in two forms: lodes or veins of gold, running vertically through underground rock, and placer deposits of gold particles that have broken away from underground veins and then have been washed, usually by floodwater, into streams, where they mixed with sand and gravel. Although lode or hard-rock gold mining contributed significantly to Virginia City's economy, placer mining far outpaced lode mining in economic return and best defines the ambience of Virginia City as a gold rush town.

With his shovel and pan next to him, a miner manipulates a rocker circa 1870 to remove gold from Alder Gulch gravel. Rockers, crude cradle-shaped boxes that trapped gold particles as water washed away the gravel, were slightly more efficient than gold pans.

According to reports by the Montana Bureau of Mines and Geology and the United States Department of Interior Bureau of Mines, about thirty million dollars of placer gold was removed from the gulch between 1863 and 1866. Mined from 1867 to 1890 was another ten million dollars of placer gold and about

Chinese miners photographed in 1871 working a sluice box in Alder Gulch.

one million dollars of lode gold. Between 1891 and 1935 the reports estimate that over eleven million dollars of placer gold and slightly more than one and a half million dollars of lode gold was realized from Alder Gulch mines.

Evidence of placer mining activity is visible the entire length of Alder Gulch, and hard-rock underground mines are found in the hills south of Virginia City. Some properties are working mines today, and many remains of closed mines are on

By the end of the 1860s streams of pressurized water coming from huge hydraulic hoses washed down hillsides and sliced cuts through ridges. The devastation shown in this circa 1870 photograph is softened today by trees and foliage growing in the cuts and hollows.

private property. Visitors driving beyond Virginia City should be aware of private land and seek permission before driving on or through it.

Although the trained eye can recognize the effects of Virginia City's mining history throughout the gulch, for the purpose of this guidebook only the remains of placer mines about one-half mile along the gulch south of Virginia City, beyond the railroad depot at the west end of Wallace Street, and on the south side of Montana Highway 287 between Virginia City and Nevada City, are described. The sites are identified on the map on page 60.

In placer mining, gold is sifted or separated from sand and gravel, which is washed away with water, leaving behind the

At the turn of the century, land was turned upside down by dredges, beyond the earlier mining sites including the first two steam dredges on either side of Alder Gulch was in the area, barely visible in the relatively undisturbed. Within a background of this photograph taken year, however, the countryside in 1900.

gold particles. Alder Gulch placer mining remains are defined by increasingly more efficient extraction methods that occurred during three time periods. From 1863 to the end of 1866 placer gold was mined with hand tools. From 1867 through the 1880s hydraulicking washed down chunks of mountainside, and, finally, from 1896 to 1941, dredge boats scooped sand and gravel from the gulch. Left behind by these three gold removal methods are mounds of dirt and gravel, ditches, reservoirs, hydraulic cuts, dredge ponds, and rock piles higher than some buildings.

The first miners to Alder Gulch panned gold, sometimes simply scooping water and sand into a pan, which they tipped slightly while swirling the water over the pan's edge to carry away the lighter weight sand and leave behind the

The crew of Conrey Placer Company's number three dredge pulls the bucket chain out of the water near Ruby in 1908. Three other kinds of dredges used in Alder Gulch were draglines, land-operated shovels that scoop gravel into recovery mechanisms floating on pontoons; dryland dredges, which power-shovel gravel into a recovery device mounted on skids or wheels; and suction dredges, which suck gravel into a washing plant.

heavier gold pieces on the pan's bottom. Most hand miners, however, shoveled gravel and sand into a rocker or cradle. Water was poured through the rocker, washing out the lighter material and capturing the heavier gold at the bottom. Sluice boxes with ridges or riffles across the bottom, which trapped the gold as water washed away the gravel, were common in the gulch. A visitor in 1865 described sluice boxes as "about two feet wide, one foot deep and from one hundred to one hundred and fifty feet high [box length measured along the incline], and given an incline of several feet in their length, so as to create a rapid current through them in order to wash away the dirt, leaving the gold free to lodge on the riffles that were nailed across their bottoms for that purpose."

Hand methods, always tedious, were especially difficult in Alder Gulch where gold deposits frequently lay twelve to twenty feet below the water's surface. To reach bedrock, miners diverted water by sinking narrow shafts through which they hauled up sand and gravel, or they dug ditches to direct water away from the claims. Some claims were on dried-up streambeds called bar or dry diggings. Because the beds were dry, bar claims were comparatively easy to mine with pick and shovel, although water then had to be conveyed to the claim to wash away the sand.

The slow, hard physical labor of hand mining was relieved with hydraulicking, which directs water through long metal hoses at high pressure, washing hillsides and gravel banks, carrying gold-bearing sand and dirt with them, into large troughs or sluices. Riffles along the trough bottom, similar to those in smaller hand sluices, trapped the gold while dirt and gravel washed away. Extensive water systems were built to carry the tremendous quantity of water required for hydraulic mining.

Hydraulicking, much more efficient than pick-and-shovel mining, was soon overtaken by dredging, which revolutionized placer mining. Dredges, resting on barges floating in a stream or pond, powered chains of buckets that revolved through the water scooping up sand and gravel from as deep as forty feet in Alder Gulch. Equipment on dredges, similar to giant sluice boxes, separated the gold from the sand and gravel, which was then dumped back onto the land. Huge piles of sand and gravel tailings and river cobbles, stones dug up from streambeds, buried older mining remains and literally obliterated the Junction and Central City mining towns as well as the western portions of Nevada City.

By following a short driving tour beginning at the corner of Jackson and Wallace streets and ending at Nevada City, visitors will see several different kinds of placer mining remains. Although most of the roads are unmarked, visitors should still be able to find the five sites noted on the driving tour map on page 60 that are representative of remains left by early hand placer mining, hydraulicking, and dredging.

DRIVING TOUR

From the corner of Wallace and Jackson streets drive south on Jackson Street just past the cattle guard to the fork shown on the map. Follow the lower or right-hand road and bear left at the next fork, for a total of one-half miles from the corner of Jackson and Wallace to the Fairweather monument (on the left side of the road). The monument marks the first strike in the gulch (site A). Low hummocky mounds of dirt and gravel overgrown by brush near the monument are typical of remains left behind by pan, rocker, and sluice hand-mining tools. Visible along the ridges on both sides of the gulch and road leading to the monument are cuts made by water gushing under high pressure from hydraulic hoses. Trees, shrubs, and bushes have taken root in the cuts tracing the line of water through the cuts from the top of the ridges to the bottom.

Turn around at the monument and drive back towards Virginia City. Just south of the fork in the road, veer slightly left onto Nevada Street and drive the short distance to the reservoir and dam at the end of Idaho Street south of the depot area (site B). Water, a necessity for gold mining, was collected and stored in reservoirs like this one, which dates

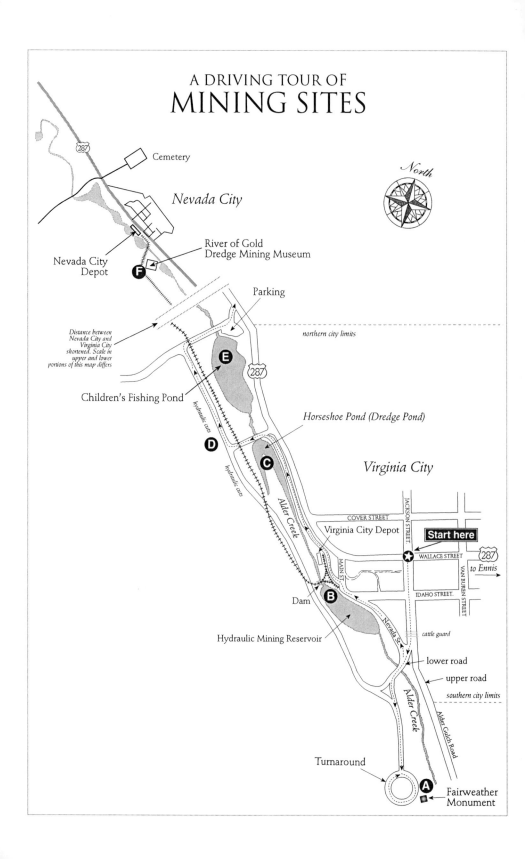

A DRIVING TOUR OF
MINING SITES

Cemetery

Nevada City

River of Gold
Dredge Mining Museum

Nevada City
Depot

F

Parking

North

*Distance between
Nevada City and
Virginia City
shortened. Scale in
upper and lower
portions of this map differs*

northern city limits

E

Children's Fishing Pond

Horseshoe Pond (Dredge Pond)

D

C

Virginia City

COVER STREET

Virginia City Depot

JACKSON STREET

Start here

287

WALLACE STREET

to Ennis

MAIN ST.

IDAHO STREET.

VAN BUREN STREET

Dam

B

hydraulic cuts

hydraulic cuts

Alder Creek

Hydraulic Mining Reservoir

Nevada St.

cattle guard

lower road

upper road

southern city limits

Alder Creek

Alder Gulch Road

Turnaround

A

Fairweather
Monument

to the late 1860s. Tracks for the narrow-gauge tourist train cross over the dam.

Veer left at the depot onto a dirt road that parallels Montana Highway 287. To the west is a horseshoe-shaped pond left by dredging operations in the 1930s. At about two-tenths of a mile past the depot turn left onto the first dirt road that curves west of Alder Gulch from the depot. Lines of trees growing up the ridge west of the road mark hydraulic cuts (site D), and large piles of cobbles on the ridge probably were removed by hand from the bottom of sluices after the water washed the dirt through the sluices, leaving the heavy stones.

After crossing the railroad tracks, turn right and drive past the children's fishing pond (site E), keeping your eyes peeled for more evidence of the gulch's mining history. Visible from the fishing hole, once a dredge pond, are piles of cobbles mixed with other placer mining debris that were dug from the gulch by dredge boats.

Turn left at the north end of the fishing pond, cross the dam, and rejoin Montana Highway 287. Turn left on 287 toward Nevada City. At the Nevada City sign, on the left side of the highway, are the remains of the *River of Gold* dredge on the grounds of the River of Gold Mining Museum (site F). Additional information about gold mining along Alder Gulch is available at the museum.

When Bill Fairweather, Henry Edgar, and their party of prospectors walked along Alder Gulch in 1863, following a route roughly paralleling the one you have just driven, they saw a far different vista from the one that engages today's travelers. One hundred and thirty-five years after Fairweather's party panned gold from the stream flowing through a natural land unturned by human hands and machinery, visitors are aware first of the upheavals of earth and rock. Although the tranquility and topography of the upper Ruby valley will never be restored to its June 1863 likeness, by looking beyond the leavings of miners and mining technology overlaying the land, visitors begin to recognize a new, emerging vista as foliage covers the rock piles, trees line the hydraulic cuts, birds and animals come to the dredge ponds, and old mining camps disappear back into a countryside that is rejuvenating itself.

Virginia City Today

⊹⇌⊹

IN PRESENT-DAY Virginia City, the lure of a gold-mining town is once again bringing people to Alder Gulch. Today it is the intrinsic value of the town as a preserved mining site, however, rather than gold itself, that attracts travelers. Fifty years after Charles and Sue Bovey initiated their campaign to save Virginia City's buildings, the 1997 Montana legislature appropriated funds to buy the Bovey properties and established a commission to work with the Montana Historical Society to manage the holdings as a historic site.

The state-owned buildings account for about one-half of the historic structures in Virginia City but one-fourth or fewer of all the buildings in the town. By legislative mandate the Montana Heritage Preservation and Development Commission, appointed by the governor and legislature, and the Montana Historical Society determine curatorial and management policies for the historic properties.

About 150 people live year-round in Virginia City, running businesses, conducting county business, and mining surrounding hills for gold, hidden still in underground veins. Another 300 summer residents service tourist needs or simply enjoy the area's offerings. The city currently occupies about 63 blocks, which hold approximately 237 major buildings. Sixteen hundred acres, including the entire town site and adjacent rural land, comprise the historic landmark.

Madison County offices are in the brick courthouse, where they have been located since 1876. Virginia City is governed by five commissioners elected to the town council, who choose the mayor from among the five sitting council members. The town's government operates from a brick schoolhouse built in 1876 to house Montana Territory's first high school. When Virginia City closed its high school in 1976 and began busing students to Ennis, fourteen miles east of Virginia City, the schoolhouse was given to the city.

Virginia City today is a working community as well as a living history museum. Visitors stay in historic hotels and residences converted to bed and breakfasts as well as in modern motels, cabins, and campgrounds. Western shops supply vintage clothing, art, books, and souvenirs. Guests relax and enjoy a variety of food and drinks in old-time saloons and restaurants. The Virginia City Players, a professional summer stock company specializing in nineteenth-century entertainment, perform at the Opera House. Special tours, museums, and the Alder Gulch Short Line, a narrow-gauge railroad between Virginia City and Nevada City, offer insights into the past. But the town's main attraction remains its historic buildings and the opportunity to mingle on the board sidewalks and to imagine oneself in the 1860s in the heart of a western mining boomtown.

Afterword
The Past Is Our Future

BY JOHN D. ELLINGSEN, *Curator of Virginia City*

VIRGINIA CITY is certainly a unique place. While the catchy phrase "frozen in time" is nearly correct, it is not perfect. Time has certainly slowed in Virginia City, but it has never quite stopped. And that may be part of the unique quality of the town that is so hard to pin down.

Virginia City has been through several major eras or periods, the first being the original gold rush, with the excitement of newfound riches both for miners and the merchants who followed them. This was also the period of the road agents' crimes, the vigilantes, and the arrival and subsequent departure of a huge population looking for free gold, but arriving too late, and moving on.

Even as thousands of disappointed gold seekers rushed to new diggings in Helena and elsewhere, Virginia City entered its second era, that of territorial capital, complete with dreams of a grand capitol building sitting in a tree-lined capitol square. Those dreams vanished when, in 1875, the capital was moved to Helena. Then Virginia City entered its third incarnation, one that lasted approximately seventy years, that of slowly declining mining town. But not a ghost town. Even though many original buildings disappeared, a core group remained occupied long enough to be saved by Charles and Sue Bovey in 1944 and 1945, just in the nick of time.

The Bovey Era was age number four. For half a century, the Boveys' presence was Virginia City's major influence. The economy turned from mining to tourism. At first baffled by Charlie Bovey's veneration of old buildings, the citizens of Virginia City eventually came to see the importance of their preservation.

The last nine years of the Bovey Era were difficult ones, fraught with worries of the loss of the buildings and their contents. But some important things happened as a result. The Dames and Moore survey, completed in 1989, listed all of the town's buildings and identified those of most significance. Architectural and historical consultants Ellen and Ken Seivert prepared a second study, individually interviewing Virginia City's entire population and discovering the community's commitment to preservation. The town council passed a very restrictive sign ordinance and an ordinance prohibiting demolition of buildings; both have become widely accepted by members of the community.

Virginia City residents' increased awareness of history has inspired many of them to participate in the Montana Historical Society's historic plaque program, and there may be more historic markers in Virginia City per capita than anywhere else in Montana. In 1995 the National Park Service held what seemed like an unending series of public meetings to test the community's feelings about preservation. The park service never ceased to be amazed at the large turnouts and the interest expressed in preserving the past. A new association, the Virginia City Preservation Alliance, joined other preservation organizations to promote and protect the town's history. These groups and thousands of individuals brought the need to preserve our heritage at Virginia City and Nevada City to the 1995 and 1997 state legislatures. And finally, on April 23, 1997, the legislature acted, buying the former Bovey properties for the citizens of Montana.

On May 16, 1997, as Ford Bovey signed the deeds for his family's properties over to the Montana Historical Society, a fifth era began, that of state ownership of the core historic properties and artifacts that have for a half century made Virginia City famous. As when people embark on any new endeavor, the events of the coming years and decades are both anticipated and feared. Concern that a "new prosperity" may bring a wealthy population to Virginia City, changing the town's character or even pricing longtime residents out of their homes, weighs heavily on many people's minds. Committed to Charlie Bovey's philosophy of preservation as a "suspended state of deterioration," many Virginia City residents fear the state might try to "sanitize history" or restore the town right out of existence. Fortunately, most of those who love Virginia City understand that future restoration needs to be "honest" to protect the credibility and continue the realism that is one of the town's major assets.

Somewhat like a crotchety old hermit prospector who has successfully ignored the changes happening in the surrounding world for most of his later life, Virginia City has developed a special life-style. Uncontrolled growth could quickly destroy the ambiance of this unusual place. Design review and zoning regulations are clearly needed to protect the special quality of this unusual town.

Despite these concerns, this newest era is one of hope and promise. The great heritage of Virginia City that survived almost by accident for eighty-two years and which the Boveys continued for the next fifty is temporarily secure. The responsibility for the future remains in our hands.

Virginia City Time Line

1804–6 Lewis and Clark Expedition

1843–46 Fort Lewis fur trade post established (renamed Fort Benton, this shipping center on the Missouri River is 235 miles north of Virginia City)

1858–59 Gold discovered in Colorado

1861–65 Civil War

July 1862 Gold discovered on Grasshopper Creek in Deer Lodge valley; Bannack (then called Bannack City) founded

March 1863 Congress creates Idaho Territory

May 1863 Fairweather/Edgar party discovers gold in Alder Gulch

June 1863 Virginia City founded

July 1863 Mining camp/towns dot Alder Gulch, including Junction, Nevada City, Central City, Highland, Pine Grove, and Summit

August 1863 A. J. Oliver and Co. begins stageline from Salt Lake City through Bannack to Virginia City

November 1863 Father Joseph Giorda conducts first church service in Virginia City

December 1863–March 1864 Vigilantes hang twenty-four men in southwestern Montana

May 1864 Congress creates Montana Territory; Organic Act creates Madison County

June 1864 President Abraham Lincoln appoints Sydney Edgerton first governor of Montana Territory

Mid-1864 Alder Gulch population estimated at 10,000; Virginia City population estimated at 5,000

July 1864 Gold discovered in Last Chance Gulch, town site of Helena

August 1864 Gold discovered in Emigrant Gulch near Yellowstone River

August 1864 John Buchanan starts the *Montana Post,* territory's first newspaper

February 1865 Capital moves to Virginia City from Bannack

February 1865 Virginia City holds first civic elections; town leaders organize Montana Historical Society in Dance and Stuart's store

Early 1865 Virginia City loses almost half its population to Helena

March 1866 Montana's first public school opens in Virginia City

November 1866 First telegraph line in Montana completed from Salt Lake City to John Creighton's store in Virginia City

March 1868 The *Montana Post* moves to Helena

1870 Census lists 867 Virginia City residents

January 1875 Territorial capital moves to Helena; Madison County seat remains in Virginia City

1880 Virginia City population drops to 634 people

December 1881 Utah and Northern Railroad reaches Butte

1885 Renewed interest in hard-rock mining brings Virginia City population back to 1,000 residents

1890 Virginia City population drops to 600

1898 Conrey Placer Mining Company opens dredging operations that continue until 1922 in Alder Gulch

1940 Census lists 380 people in Virginia City

1942 Congress declares precious metal mining a nonessential industry for the war effort and issues Gold Mine Closing Order, stopping all mining in Virginia City

1944 Charles and Sue Bovey first visit Virginia City, begin efforts to preserve historic structure

1945 Charles Bovey buys Henry N. Blake house, Bovey's first Virginia City acquisition

1961 Virginia City designated National Historic Landmark

1976 Virginia City nominated to National Register of Historic Places

1997 State of Montana purchases Bovey Properties in Virginia City

Suggested Reading

_{+>=<+}

Guide to Historic Virginia City is heavily dependent on the State Historic Preservation Office survey conducted by Dames and Moore. Copies of Paul D. Friedman's "Final Report of the Architectural, Historical and Archaeological Inventory of the Virginia City National Historic Landmark Madison County, Montana" (Denver: Dames and Moore, 1990) are available through the State Historic Preservation Office, Montana Historical Society, in Helena.

OTHER VALUABLE REFERENCES INCLUDE:

Barsness, Larry. *Gold Camp*. New York: Hastings House, 1962.

Cushman, Dan. *Montana—The Gold Frontier*. Great Falls: Stay Away Joe Publishing, 1973.

Dimsdale, Thomas. *The Vigilantes of Montana*. 1866. Reprint, Norman: Oklahoma University Press, 1953.

Graves, F. Lee. *Bannack: Cradle of Montana*. Helena: American and World Geographic Publishing, 1991.

Howard, Joseph Kinsey. *Montana High, Wide, and Handsome*. 1943. Reprint, Lincoln: University of Nebraska Press, 1983.

Langford, Nathaniel P. *Vigilante Days and Ways*. 1890. Reprint, Missoula: University of Montana Press, 1957.

Malone, Michael P., Richard B. Roeder, and William L. Lang. *Montana: A History of Two Centuries*. 1976. Rev. ed., Seattle: University of Washington Press, 1991.

Pace, Dick. *Golden Gulch: The Story of Montana's Fabulous Alder Gulch*. Virginia City: Virginia City Trading Co., 1970.

Rifkind, Carole. *A Field Guide to American Architecture*. New York: The New American Library, 1980.

Sievert, Ken, and Ellen Sievert. *Virginia City and Alder Gulch*. Helena: American and World Geographic Publishing, 1993.

Spence, Clark C. *The Conrey Placer Mining Company*. Helena: Montana Historical Society Press, 1989.

Stuart, Granville. *The Montana Frontier, 1852–1864*. 1925. Reprint, Lincoln: University of Nebraska Press, 1977.

Index of Building Sites

LaVergne, TN USA
13 April 2010
179087LV00001B/1/P